Bright Stranger

Louisiana State University Press   Baton Rouge

poems

Bright Stranger

Katherine Soniat

Published by Louisiana State University Press
Copyright © 2016 by Katherine Soniat
All rights reserved
Manufactured in the United States of America
LSU Press Paperback Original
First printing

DESIGNER: *Mandy McDonald Scallan*
TYPEFACE: *Trade Gothic, display; Whitman, text*

Many thanks to the editors of the following journals in which these poems first appeared:

Amicus Journal: "August Annals" and "Perspective"; *Amicus 30 Anniversary Anthology:* "August Annals"; *Anthology of Southern Poetry: Louisiana:* "Easter Inventory" and "One of the First Questions"; *Antioch Review:* "After a Day at Bussard's Farm" and "Dark and Secret Kin"; *Asheville Poetry Review:* "Epithalamion" and "Filings"; *Chariton Review:* "Bright Stranger," "Eurydice Turning," and "The Essential Eurydice"; *Connotations Press: Congeries:* "In a Fish-Blue Surround" (titled "Commerce); *Crazyhorse:* "Aerial Photo-Ops of the Biome," "Anise," and "Point, Line, and Plane"; *Cut Throat:* "Dodge/Luhan, Works in Progress"; *Denver Quarterly:* "Ellipse," "Eros," "Mitosis," and "Open House"; *Florida Review:* "The Forest People"; *Hotel Amerika:* "Blood Roses," "Burnt October," "Earth Flashed *Fire Here*," "Easter Inventory," "Hubris," "Things that Hang in the Air" (titled "Brilliance); *Image: Art, Faith, and Mystery:* "Happiness"; *Mad Hat Review:* "Materialism," "Talk of Winter," and "The Volga"; *Mid-American Review:* "A History of Religion," "Phenomenology with a Future," and "Shade"; *Pine Mountain Sand and Gravel: Anthology of Appalachian Writing:* "*Green* is a Word" (titled "Still"); *Roanoke Review:* "What Else There Is To Do"; *Superstition Review:* "Power Lines"; *Turtle Island Quarterly:* "Arrival"; *Tiferet:* "Fuzz" and "Homeward" (titled "Return"); *Women's Review of Books:* "Burnt October"; *World Poetry Portfolio #60:* "A Light Sleeper" (titled "Like This").

Library of Congress Cataloging-in-Publication Data

Names: Soniat, Katherine, author.
Title: Bright stranger : poems / Katherine Soniat.
Description: Baton Rouge : Louisiana State University Press, [2016]
Identifiers: LCCN 2015035399| ISBN 978-0-8071-6241-5 (pbk. : alk. paper) | ISBN 978-0-807-16242-2 (pdf) | ISBN 978-0-8071-6243-9 (epub) | ISBN 978-0-8071-6244-6 (mobi)
Classification: LCC PS3569.O65396 A6 2016 | DDC 811/.54—dc23
LC record available at http://lccn.loc.gov/2015035399

The paper in this book meets the guidelines for permanence and durability of the Committee on Production Guidelines for Book Longevity of the Council on Library Resources. ∞

for my good teachers

What I am saying is hard to tell and harder to understand unless you have been to the edge of Deep Canyon and come back unharmed. Maybe it depends on something within you . . . whether you are trying to see Watersnake or sacred Cornflower—whether you go out to meet death or Seek Life.
—SAN JUAN PUEBLO ELDER

One reason why geometry is often described as "cold and dry" lies in its inability to describe the shape of a cloud, a mountain, a coastline, or a tree. Clouds are not spheres, mountains are not cones, coast lines are not circles, and bark is not smooth, nor does lightning travel in a straight line. Nature exhibits not simply a higher degree but an altogether different level of complexity.
—BENOIT MANDELBROT, *The Fractal Geometry of Nature*

Contents

i. *study night and the river   as if they hold the twin of all that disappeared*

Shade 3
Green is a Word 4
Hunger 5
Talk of Winter 6
A History of Religion 7
August Annals 8
Anise 9

ii. *create volume and depth   like you're sending them to a friend   who's never felt such before*

Happiness 13
Phenomenology with a Future 14
Power Lines 15
Filings 16
What Else There Is To Do 17
After a Day at Bussard's Farm 18
Things that Hang in the Air 21

iii. *one can look years for the right   meaning of departure*

Arrival 25
The Volga 26
Open House 27
Eurydice Turning 28
The Essential Eurydice 29
Eros 32
Ellipse 33

iv.   *no one to track.   The hours and miles*
       spent circling disappearance   like a canyon

Bright Stranger
    1. asylum   37
    2. a beginning   38
    3. river   39
    4. strata   41
    5. mantra   42
    6. apocrypha   44
    7. inquiry   46

v.   *deep calleth unto deep even to the dancing waterspout. And*
       there a house spins round like home again

In a Fish-Blue Surround   49
Homeward   50
One of the First Questions   51
Easter Inventory   53
Dodge/Luhan, Works in Progress   56
Materialism   57
The Forest People   58

vi.   *such a baffled look as the beast lay stepped from.   Almost*
        forgotten

Mitosis   61
Dark and Secret Kin   62
Burnt October   63
The Earth Flashed, *Fire Here*   66
Hubris   67
Black Roses   69
Perspective   70

vii.   *who cares if the mouth has a beak   or bells in the throat*

The Silence 73
A Light Sleeper 74
Coastal Epithalamion 75
Fuzz 76
Simplicity 77
Aerial Photo-Ops of the Biome 78
Point, Line, and Plane 79

Manuscript Note

As the spectral figures—Orpheus and Eurydice—appeared in the depths of Hell, so too they walk in and out of poems in *Bright Stranger*. Recall that myth of "the father of song" and his bride Eurydice. On their wedding day she steps into a nest of snakes that mortally wound her. Orpheus, upon finding her body in the tall grasses, follows her descending spirit to the Underworld. Responding to the beauty and sadness of Orpheus' lament, Hades promises the lovers safe passage back to the Upper World on one condition: Orpheus must walk in front of his wife, and not look back. But turn he does, and for a second time Eurydice is sent silently to that realm of darkness, forever.

i. *study night and the river   as if they hold
the twin of all that disappeared*

Shade

I tracked it through branches, then deeper into the woods,
these flickering variances in green. Splices of sunlight
we measure time by.
                        Early water clock, the way it turned
the molecules to logic. Chirp of seconds—our need
to always know what time it is
growing strong.

Shade clock. Sundial. Brass pendulum with its propensity
to fall toward earth again.

The gravity of time,

seconds that tock and tick and trick us into thinking
water's the same twice.   Study night and the river
as if they hold the twin of all that disappeared.

I've felt through shadows in the dirt, and wanted
to be like that. Dark and humid.
A lowness,
        not these passing thoughts, my questions
answered by minutiae. Equivocation—headlights
blur along the ridge, travelers caught in fog.

Years ago I held a match to glyphs in a limestone cave, then
walked the old path down to the river. At noon it stopped
by water.
        That's when I floated facedown on the current—
my body offering anonymity to each small thing below.

Green Is a Word

I haven't thought of lately. Bread and jam,
the carbs that move me and make my stomach
churn. Turds, I find along the canyon path, another
animal clue left behind. Territory marked—saturated
fur snagged on rock. Black talons, half-buried in the
ground, suggest detached waiting or dying where the
body dropped.
                    Before me spreads a human story—
cellophanes of candy and talk enough to numb
the brain, blind it to clear-cutting and how the
empty eyes of miners stare while magma shifts
Earth's tectonic plates—an underworld on the
move again.
                    Who cares about collapse? Guys
on mules make a game of yelling their way down
to the canyon floor.
                    And, not another word about
women alone. They tsk, tsk, then nail me with, *Oh
dear, you've been left behind*, spotting a man and boy
on the trail ahead. Even a friend at home took
swipes at solitude . . . *but you must talk to someone
while you're gone*, dismayed how soon I shed
my human tongue. Hikers mill about on
the promontory. Condor watches us
coagulate and separate, alert for
carrion stillness.

Hunger

condor
spots
deadcalm
the lowdown
carrion body
(not a breath)
wait and see
its poised
pose of death
a fastidious
hunger—
head
neck
naked
as ever
so gutsy
parasites
won't stick
and afterwards
swoosh unwieldy
bird flies high for
snowmelt to splash
each slick fold clean
then positions
stillness
again

Talk of Winter

Delirium of broken placenta,
snow on the path makes her ride home
clandestine.

Quiet.

Sleigh   the sort that wolves can't leave alone.

Teeth snap in her sleep.
                            Organs, a ripe darkness on ice.

Then dreams of the panther in bed, its paws
on both her shoulders.

Wet winter smell of big cat. The two of them
breathing.
            A strange place to end up.
Surrender.

Who said, *Don't be afraid to show how it started?*

. . . island covered by sleet, and afterwards they never
could get each other out of the blood. His.   Hers,
while the ghost capillaries trade oxygen back
and forth.

Thin blue storylines inflate.

She bit her tongue, and it was still his blood in her mouth.
Sap in the maples froze. Talk of strata and winter sadness

under a delicately pricked roof.

Ping, ping,   ice on tin.

Time, unreasoned and amorphous.

A History of Religion

And it came to pass
                       she too was called "no more
than a self-absorbed, neurotic slut."

Thus began the old decline of flesh to language—
                       something of the accused, the distrusted
tossed to a crowd ready with stones. Heaven on earth she was,
which was understandable considering only a small percentage
of Americans surveyed think heaven will be boring.

August Annals

A window holds the blue containment of noon,
and every day the dog trots into it, pees on the clover,

then makes headway through the Timothy grass,
his coat full of seed. He has some idea of where to go

and who wants him. And since he's no skeptic, he goes—
rye, corn, the whole fermenting season ablaze,

a dog running off as if to make August history.

Who's to say his is not the lithe world that swayed
around pharaoh's daughter and the baby
in the bulrushes.

And this same sun overhead heated the earth when voices flared
a final, frantic time for Joan on her pyre of wood. Exact, those
moments in the reeds or staked above the fiery sticks, while
a dog flops down after hours of futile adventure, the ravine
filled with wings and an undergrowth of eyes.

Anise

Rainwater, lamplight, and *anise* are words I wake with
one snowy spring morning.
                              Or is it *light rain* and *lamp water*—
surely there was *anise,* the other two uncertain as March melt.

Rachmaninoff's *Elegiac Piano Trio* plays from last night,
dictionary open by the window where sparrows peck the ice for seed.
Beneath black branches the yard glistens.

Perhaps this is when anise should enter from the Adriatic, syllables
of "yellow floral whorls near the spice-scented sea." It's too cold
for *rain-light* to haunt my mirror, and far from here *water lamps*
whiten a flounder in the shallows.

Today the calendar is right for an afternoon of anise cakes and votive lights
on Saint Joseph's Day altars in courtyards of parish churches. That's when
we stuffed our dirty pockets full, then ran home for supper.

Rachmaninoff leans into his piano: *lento lugubre* settles into *largo*.

Sharps and flats surround my cat at the window, fur like orange frost.

Fading little lion.

ii. *create volume and depth   like you're sending them
to a friend   who's never felt such before*

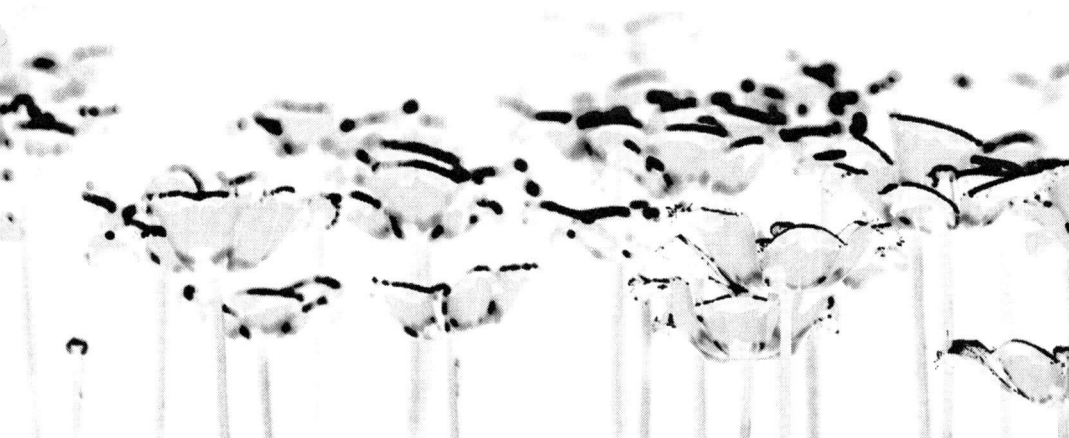

Happiness

She painted her nails metallic rose at night,
placed the opal on her finger, then walked
down the block to a party in the moss garden.
A friend held her hand, getting involved
with the milky luminescence
of the ring.

Before long he was telling her how his uncle
loved to float in the river with a favorite cow.
And indeed that bovine figure was a fabled
swimmer.
                The water had a bluish tint, swirling
slowly through summer. The cow with a hoop in its nose
for the rope swam alongside the man. This uncle, who had lived
alone his whole life, often spoke of this cow. By some accounts,
both could be seen as flying.

Phenomenology with a Future

> Language is the perpetual oscillation between homeland and exile.
> —GIORGIO AGAMBEN

When she turned forty, he gave her Hegel's *History of Philosophy*
and *The Communist Manifesto*, then tossed in that she had the personal
insight of Byron in a sand storm.

Such a fine assembly of rhetoric and persona to fall in with. And all
the while she was thinking it was likely Montana would save her
as she lifted mirrors from the wall.

Once there, that nasty habit of seeing herself in everything, and vice versa,
would be buried in snow. And if not, there'd be plenty sky to dissolve
into, horse-whisperers the only pedants for miles.

Power Lines

Had those stockings not slipped from her legs in the small
hours of the morning,
                        there would not have been her hair
undone for him to touch like a favored summer doll.

Now she reads the account,
his metered frames of (how he framed) her.

Multiple exposures of night on a bed.

His what-he-says-she-said.
                        Those lines,
and the spaces between.

Space: galaxies collapse as he decides he was taken in.
Line: ". . . of her men, I know that bed best."

His last line, a rhyme—"joined at the groin"—
surgical at best.

Filings

By fall, what had been
disappeared behind curtains,
balled up under the bed or park bench for the winter.

There's an art to not connecting. The moment dispensed with,
language cauterized.

Nothing extended.

The mouth is a hollow cave—adding a tongue shapes syllables
but not wonder.

Their story wasn't to be concluded or discounted, so the fall
forward seemed interminable.
                                    Point of view faltered.

She tried to focus on the man who, oddly enough, appeared to be
listening—his eyes, the knit brow.

Alphabet letters spun in a basket, flashing combinations of what
had made sense.

The Periodic Chart does not show time-lapse between discoveries. Space,
then innovation. And, indeed, years passed between the symbol for helium
(peelings of sunlight) and one for iron (rock, our bloodied bodies).

The breakup finally was laughingly referred to as the autopsy. Severance,
then the hissing sputtered loose. Neither of them (one acting dead
by then) thought much of time anymore.

His voice rose from the phone (deep vortex), one of their last connections.
Rule 1-3: neither mouth nor eyes (or body for that matter) should touch.
Otherwise, the two of them might carry on at length from day to day

from pole to pole

headlights coming from the wrong direction

What Else There Is To Do

Because the earth spins round and our lives are wired,
we don't hear the slow drip of rain
from the eaves.

Bell in the breeze, missed.

So we say we're busy thinking
thoughts that multiply and reinvent themselves. Lips stretch
to a smile, or turn down with menace on bad days.

Maintain a glimmer of yourself running through the hourglass.
In the middle of a starry galaxy, you might look down

through miles of wonder.

Try rubbing your cheek on bark of a tree, then waiting
like the jaguar whose nose is said to be uncanny.

One summer morning, the man who had a profound stutter
was heard speaking fluently to the lion in the zoo, while a deaf
girl at school wanted most to live in a sea-cave with her drum.

After a Day at Bussard's Farm

During the first class my father was asked to comment
on his drawings to better understand the subtleties of
charcoal and a rubber eraser. The course description
made it clear that creating from memory was expected,
and for his final self-portrait a transparency of the human
skull would be used as an overlay.

The necessity for experiment, the instructor emphasized counted
more than a student's ability to analyze or evaluate. Though
the human eye sees both creatively and abstractly, most find
only the latter. That's what his teacher had to say about Basics
of Drawing taught at the community college in the suburbs
of D.C.

At times, the concepts he copied into his sketchbook read
like a parallel history. Two points eventually refer to a third,
that being the vanishing point: From his destroyer, he'd seen
men caught in the crosshairs explode on the Pacific. Flares
of color. Refractions, like the great Crab Nebulae.
Then nothing.

One Saturday in his study, he decided the assignment was more
than he could manage. Bookshelves, chairs, his desk on the red
braided rug. *Rearrange a familiar grouping. Draw it.* In the notebook
is written *etc. etc. etc.* replacing any attempt at design. Otherwise,
the page, dated October 25, is blank.

Then it was time to work from memory: *Preferably, a figure represented
by frames of action, the dimensions blocked off. Picture a single energy running
through your subject on which all else depends.* Each of his figures appear from a
different angle of arrest.

My father found inspiration on the top shelf of the hall closet.
Drawing after drawing of his herring-bone cap and gabardine scarf,
items that always were there when I opened the door—my first book
of poems tossed with maps on the floor. He found comfort in things
above ground and inland, preferred whistling to speech.

By Thanksgiving he noted the following techniques needed his attention:
More middle-tones such as grays and lavender. Boundaries are too distinct.
Professor says, *create volume and depth like you're are sending them
to a friend who never has felt such.*

When the nude arrived to sit on the table by a window, his drawings
disappear. Confused by the difference between the contour of a breast
and its outline, he eliminates the woman completely, asking *if she
were a thing created for (or by) his imagination to express an
inexplicable . . . ?* Inexplicable is firmly underlined.
The noun never appears.

Week 12: The egg. His pink eraser smudges the oval shell.
The chamois and fingers are tools of softness now. Edges
blurred with rubbery dust. *Scuro:* dark. *Chiaro:* light.
New words for the night.

Week 13: Egg grows more opulent and cross-hatched, bottom
like a nest in the reeds.

Notes on a visit to the museum to see Brueghel's art, end of the term:
*other than a few handwritten letters, sketches, and his paintings,
not much of him survives. No contacts. No correspondences.*
Wizard of autobiography, deletion, I think. Then somehow
he gets this idea—*there are few works by Brueghel that one
can look at seriously, without laughing.* Without irony,
he writes it down.

For the final project, he has the choice of his self-portrait (15x20)
with the overlay of skull. Or he can mat and frame a favorite image
of himself. Neither is present. There are several sketches of a skull.
The first, a profile, is weak-chinned and doubles as it sits on a mirror
beside the milk bottle and jar of baby-food.

Then the semester is over, and he's alone and drawing randomly. Brief
forays to/attempts at Bussard's Farm. Three trees. Under one a headless
figure, and weeks later spidery outlines of a pier with boats tied to it,
then crossed out. Scrawled below in cursive, *Too Frustrating.*
A final entry.

In the last pages of his book   my words are written—

May/milepost 171   daughter/the name afforded me
listing birds   binoculars (x735):

white-eyed vireo   mimics

cowbird   lays eggs in others' nests

catbird   the mocker

barn owl   repeats the *who-who*   two short
three long   diffidently

rufous towhee   *drink-your-tea,   drink-your-tea*
rising from the russian olive

song sparrow   best of their kind do not travel well
shipped far across the ocean

hushed   the one who found whistling easier than words

Things that Hang In the Air

Fermata is the musical notation either to sustain a note or
      pause for a duration longer than the indicated time.

Expanse of sky, our boat under the stars—anything possible with pen
and paper. Now I'm busy erasing a triangulation of boat and stars. One

of the former, two the latter. Rocking on water makes me want to smear
the fiery dots, and be no party to loss. Dead reckonings. Me, entitled

to nothing beneath the stars.   And even if it was years ago on a lake—
cyclical sway of the tides, fish nudging our ankles—we swam under

loose arrangements.   Scorpius.   Ursa Major.
Beasts of perception, not of starlight.   Imposed too, that musical

notation to hold silence longer   or extend the score.   Double edge
of the *fermata*   like wordless Eurydice whose thoughts carried on

past the story.   How long she shut up, shut down in hell, Hades
her composer.   Calls for lost children sometimes drift across

the water. Their names vibrant after each milky scent goes cold. Echo
of what never quite ends.   One step followed by the next—the path

through loss known finally.   Who understands what *temporary*
means anyhow? Time has its own sign language. Glass-bottom boat,

one arrested vision after another. Then a flashcard flick of   *I have
nothing more to say.* A whole person   exhaled   excluded

in a phrase. Words left out.   That kind of ending.   How many
are not heard of again in this life   or any other?   And what

silence can do   it does—initial frame of the female *fermata*. My
family in childhood.   Mutes settled with bourbon in the garden.

Dwarfs in bed until morning.   And between each tick of the
clock   silence.   Blitz of autumn fermatas.

iii.   *one can look years for the right   meaning of departure*

Arrival

Eclipse crawls another silvery ball.
Black, some say, equals simplicity,
a lack of empathy—the way my student wanted
"nature to be straightforward, all those dumb personifications
set aside. After all, it's just a place where the animals eat each other up."

Soon I'll have the moon to myself
and need to move on.
Me, my own
pawn in the where-to.

Once I was sure of something.
The Russian port of Murmansk
had an animal that sounded like it,
and then I recalled *marmot*.
In that mouthful lived what I'd been looking for,
not furry particularity, but the yearning out
of *ahs* and *ohs*   Space before a word
comes for mountain

One can look years for the right meaning of departure
The dog howls after the car drives away
He waits under the tree   his protest
its own arrival

The Volga

As a youth Chagall stared at barnyard animals
from his attic window, then beyond them
to the Volga.

Perhaps, in a like frame of mind, my student
writes in his journal, *I move beyond time and space,
and mostly think of Sex. Who cares how close the source
of laughter, sneeze, and orgasm are?*

I read this while the incense burns, smoke not the least
concerned with conclusion. Could each beginning
rise if we let it?
                      Take this painting by the master,
the one of a sleigh high in midnight blue. In it sits
a man, woman, and their baby ready to nurse.
The nipple is red and overly upright, gravity
dissolved at such altitude. Harnessed,
a giant rooster pulls them through
the stars. How far below churns
the Volga?

Open House

That night I took you as final, as done—
one more restlessness turned out to steam in the woods.

It hurt to look outdoors. The pine ridge roughened,
the stream came to less the cows lapped from,
apples thumped the ground.

A bluing.
Morning grew pale and thick with extraction.

A bodily decision, I let myself down into a tub of hot,
hot water.　　　　　Ankles, knees, then up to my neck

where sorrow brimmed and broke like a long line

of creatures fallen   heart pumping with come and

come again　　　　Vast invitation

Eurydice Turning

How diminished she was after settling
for the underworld—a malcontent

in Hades' household, her thoughts unspoken.
That sibilant *shhhh, shhhh, Eurydice*—like

an owl's *who-who* at dusk in the branches
of another life. Here there's neither night nor day.

No break, no brokered hours. Only an unwinding
spool of gray. Some dismayed Shade must have

stuck a hook in Eurydice's mouth, whispering,
do not speak or swallow. Weak-muscled tongue,

a dying thing. She knew when Orpheus looked
around what would be exacted, her future spun

to cosmic reckoning.   No reason why.
Nothing left finally but his singing, floating head

and she, silent creature accompanied by her body.
Buttocks and hips that sway like death in the saddle.

Spectral too, those wild Maenads who killed Orpheus
for not rolling naked with them by the river. At night

she dreams other women's fury. Fate bows and steps
aside.   Half female and fish, she's subterranean

with the blind albino eyes.   Cavern silt, gill slit, and
cold skin—she's lashed to the mind of Orpheus,

his backward glance.

The Essential Eurydice

(*pattern*)   First time down   I was still
seeing snakes and weddings—

the route to hell endless.

Then descent was mine again   until
and suddenly   like pounds of flesh

I fell back to Hades.   As one clamped
to an ocean floor   my legs a thing apart.

Was there wind and light above?   More
a likelihood than not—waves blowing green

and lucid.   And Orpheus

～

Such dreams I had   plotting
ways back to our meadow.   My return

set finally for midsummer on a day that
would not happen.

(*props*)   wilderness of candle in my head—
small sun   the Earth tilting from solstice

to solstice

~

(reitieration) The net a voice can cast. I heard
the moment he thought *lover.*

Predictable my low echo.
                    Sad   Orpheus
had no kerchief for his eyes as I followed him
toward daylight—there'd have been

no need for turning

~

(*chiaroscuro*)   A brain twists by the fire
in hell.   Mica sparkles   and with it

shadows of another home.   Half-life
of the half-asleep—tired Penelope

but without her wide Aegean

~

(*invitation*) Try to breathe in the underworld my mythic
friends and the tender parts go dry. Bite a fragrance

you think full of summer   then spit the seed.
Nostrils pull tight as purse strings.   My hands

callous with thoughts of touching.   So   take time
to eat your heart out   but chew slowly

~

What's lost becomes a tarnished shining.   A shambling
heavier than mountains.   Undeliverable

Horsemen motion in the trees.　　　　And pass, we did,
a pair of bound contradictions.

(*chorus*)　　Sing *Orpheus*　but keep your back to her.
Death   waits on its proud white stallion

　　　　　　　　　　　～

(*silence*)　　　　　　　　　　　Amnesia is a time
without history.　　　　　The quickest route to vanishing.

Thought ripped away　　　　　　　　currents clotted.
The animals step back　　and back　　　soon to be

backed off the planet.　　Somewhere in the woods' frail
mix　　the huff of re-creation.　　　　　The world

speaks in tongues again—*fish-woman*　　*merman*　　*minotaur*
and *satyr*　　　　Raucous in the bushes　　Pan

Primordial celebration

　　　　　　　　　　　～

(*stillness*)　　Sleight of hand　a shift in gravity　　and I leave
this body behind　　　　　　　　I'll choose my shape

and when to disappear from any cave　　　　or canyon
Ultimate fade　　　　of the woman he moved beside

in a wet inverted place　　　　　　　　her ocean

Eros

A solitary place
this planet

some think has nothing to do with them.

They don't sense kindred furred Vs of motion
and moisture, nor do they embrace for long

one point in the arch cataclysm of stars.

Only at night, a few find themselves naked
and alone from the start.

Ellipse

It wasn't a question of uncertain periphery
or surface density. There was no occlusion
to the heart since birth or end
implied
        only a record of your early breathing
and who you were and had been for decades
that no longer added up.

There was this   your singularly directed act
overwhelming what I knew.

                And the speed at which you left.

You—my son   going for dead center
then straight down
head first
through any thing on earth that might oppose you.

I stood on the rim   raw with possibilities.

Proof of nothing

but convergence when the collapsing spheres of Euclid
almost had you—so ready were they to erase any shifty
human form.

iv.   *no one to track.   The hours and miles*
       spent circling disappearance   like a canyon

Bright Stranger

1. asylum
>—North Rim (8,000 ft.) facing Red Butte. Transept Trail.

On the north side of this ancient dwelling (only a stone or two high
by now), I sit after dreaming of my office mate last night: Two of us

in our own cramped cubicle separated by the backless bookcase,
unsteady ladder of glory-be-to-the-brain.   Pink and sprinkled

with quartz are the stones in this makeshift foundation: 5' x 17'.
I paced it off, lodged it in my mind, and at center are remnants

of another wall. Another crumbled attempt at solitude, one rock
layer, then another—high summer shelter from long ago for

humans to sleep inside.   A woman passing on the trail
mutters, *Just face it*, as her man slumps into, *I guess you're right*,

and neither see the flares of canyon light.   Resin glistens in a
pine—ruts where lightning leapt up a tree. While above,

that old sapsucker sun keeps shining.   In my rucksack right now
I find the card marked Sky-Credit for the miles we once crossed.

Rivers, villages, and mountains.   Those words are arced
by a rainbow and three commercial stars offering a ticket to some-

where else.   Always, another time than now. *Credit*, the promise
to savor.   *Vintage credit*, I think, strings of imagined coasts,

our reward for delay. Everything stored for the future.   And only
months ago, fox maiden danced in canyon heat—glimpse of fur

and flame in the branches.   Fox on the loose,   fanning the blaze
with her tail.   No plans   or energy to save.

Clicking her teeth, the sparks fly.   A forest on fire

2. a beginning

                  When counting backwards, spring birth means autumn
rutting. Auburn fur caught in barbed wire across the fire road out to Lovers Pointe.
                Fox barks in the canyon.
Clouds shadow the river.

So, why this remains of a central wall in such a small dwelling? Two groups of
bodies given cover for nights.   Not as solitaries, these people migrated to the rim
for summer, moon shining into crevices and gorges
known as the ancestor's land.

How many embryos floated loose inside this canyon? Androgynous shapes, organs
not yet complete in the amniotic pool.   A boat prepared
for each to cross the water.
                            The raft midway to rest upon.   And westward,
a rainbow bridge from temple to temple—Zoroaster, Shiva, and Brahma
—those red rock spires that point out the heavens

3. river

female   scooped   by current and quartz.

Purple clouds
and hawk filled with the cries of broken glass.

For those who take note and are (sinking by the minute)
passing away
               there's the North Star to be clear about
from below.

The mind   salient and lucid

recalls the white horse in snow for what it was,
the rooster at dawn as no other.

Point and counterpoint.   The journey.

                         A song sparrow
sat beside me a moment ago, turning a cup of tea
to warm vibration.   Filling it.

There's little sadness when the traveler departs.
Stones are cold that circled his fire.   After all,
who's the one that said, *Look at me or be done*,
and stood up in the boat?

Something to consider—that pearl on the night horizon,
and how we'll not pass this way again.

Quiet drifting river, no fingers to trail north this trip.

Clips of a life.

And cross-eyed with prescience—double-vision of the wise—
he whispered, *Let's sleep on it   and see what dreaming
brings*
        That far away from the present   Implausible
faults   crooked seas   Whitewashed faces

Oars in an empty boat

4. strata

A pinon pine grows beside the ruins, alive
as shadows on the canyon wall—silhouettes

that grow longer by the minute. Then, those
red spires at sundown. I look from here to

there, way over there, then back to my hand.
A view supported by nothing. Much like the

vellum envelope addressed in dream by my lover,
and delivered at dark: I sniff the glue,   open it

to find a blank page.   No words to speak of this
time. Only seven white tablets, lots of Ambien,

and an invisible prescription for whiskey with breakfast.
Unlimited refills.   But I am hearing something else

skitter around in that envelope when a woman with her
red fanny pack pulls me back to the canyon, asking

if *a bunch of* silly *dwarfs lived inside this teensy place.*
Her son looks indifferent, batting bugs in the sun. Maybe

he too will receive shocks from the other side,
a smoke signal at a time. One puff for white mystery

pills, three from Ambien which combined with daily
whiskey add up to a man I once loved who passed from

the picture.   All these layers of lives make me wonder
how many bones lay within the strata—another way of

reading history.   Take that day I saw half of what might
have been a crow, and let it go like that   So the bridges

sway   news from the vertical universe

5. mantra

I bet you'll miss my presence in the dark, my son
said. But whose darkness was this anyway—

his or mine?   More to that dream than I could
possibly know. The unthinkable arrives however

the mind wraps around it.   Shiva, Brahma, and
friends rose unnoted from the canyon floor. First

I saw them from a promontory far away.   My take
on what once were corals anchored among the rosy

clownfish.   Oceanic fossils bathed now in light.
But stay with these heights, with the awful vertigo

of not knowing to whom the dark belongs: something
dimly suggested in the sadness of clowns. Smile of

the gay-faced and somber. Deeper than somber,
the knowledge I'll carry to the next life.   If I go

through that again, I'll recognize trumpets and how
 the grand entrance begins with brasses on a clear day

in Monteverdi's *L'Orfeo*—that opera-opening celebratory,
except for brief interludes of quiet—of *just-be-still-and-breathe*

while waiting for the merry notes. And indeed, my son
would find the moist blessing of one breath taken, and

another.   But not   then: Who suspected the future
that July sunrise in the woods? I sat on a log and did not

understand the chatter of leaves beneath a fox's feet.
Burnt russet streaming before me, its white-tipped tail.

This fox, my dead husband's nickname, re-embodied in
fresh   thick fur   :   :   Father-ghost in disguise

days before our son's immanent departure   Abrupt
ruthless as the human mind could make it   Wind blew

in four directions   No pattern to make sense of   I was nine
days out from retrospect   Only that lit red fur

in a void I could not fathom
Me and this animal so close   Cross-talk between the species

Repeat, say who you thought you were that morning

among the trees.

6. apocrypha

Can a voice in dream be spectral   before passing
to the other side?

That dream paused after my son's bet surrounding
the word *dark*—wondering who owns it,
and why.
          Like hoping the sun and moon will fail,
so one won't diminish the other.   That slant
of thinking.

Stripped logic.   Screw that does not hold.

Nothing can be excluded from the subterranean
thoughts of another—

brains of the children we make, their decisions
that destroy us.

Conceivers   step up

keeners

across time.

Lost children have fathers too—men touched deeply   at the beginning
can reappear near the end:
                              One morning a fox walked
from the bushes   Drift of July light   And within days the sleep-messenger
came making guesses   throwing dice in the air   After that
the hourglass began to run out   to run dry   Punch a hole in the breath—
and nothing's left to tear   No one to track
The hours and minutes   spent circling disappearance
like a canyon

                    Hands flew off the clock until the-life-not-taken
(almost androgynous by then) walked from its cave Eyes as big as combat
Doorway of a cheap motel   Beckoning me   he
(. . . for *he* was mine   thus limited again)   put a finger to his lips
and that door shone bright around him Truck gears shifted across arteries
of a city   *It didn't have to be like this* I thought   then thought again
knowing Eurydice never made it back

7. inquiry

Who was the uninvited guest who followed another
down, and returned?

A kept secret.

And did your finger to the lips mean *hush*, no words
or spoken tongues will ever capture this one?

And had Swenson expected an answer when she wrote,

how will it be to lie in the sky / without roof or door / and

the wind for an eye . . . how will I hide?

v.   *deep calleth unto deep even to the dancing waterspout.   And there a house spins round like home again*

In a Fish-Blue Surround

Blue heron stands on the tidal flats. Before it the Atlantic swells, and
    before that the Earth spun round for ages, our galaxy curled in a spiral.

Feathery mosaics ripple on water. Birds wade the sunny side of the planet,
    autumn blowing sand across Route 6. I walk the shore toward town,

to the commerce of tip your eyes up, or down to the next passerby, while
    the season with a hungry mouth never gets enough. Surf sucks seaweed

from under the pier. Half-empty is half-full, or so the tides imply. And
    there's my reflection holding clouds in the sky. Blank bluster of me

at my feet in the shallows—a body fitted with legs and filled with motion.
    The pleasure of thinking it makes a whole hell of a difference,

these mindless gyrations of *who's who, me first,* and *who cares about
    the homing plight of birds.* A dog shakes off sand then runs up Pearl St.

to Dinah's Kitchen.   We plan in terms of destination, dream of polar
    opposites.   The street vendor lifts high the I'm-Worth-More-Money-

Than-You Doll. She whines this when he pulls her string. On town square,
    her livelier versions mill around with bright scarves, chocolates with the

liquid center.   The pulse of I'll buy this one, you that, until the proper
    image is struck—beer served under lights of cinnabar, driftwood priced

with flames that go with sunset. What flies off with the spirit at dawn,
    leaving faint prints in the sand?   I dream sleek loops in a fish-blue

surround where the voice sings, *deep calleth unto deep, even to the
    dancing waterspout:* And there a house spins round like home again,

blur of my old porch and curtains.   Then down it falls into daybreak,
    into the off-season.   Heron asleep in the marsh.

Homeward

> Come, and come again, whoever you are . . .
> wanderers, worshipers, lovers of leaving.
> —RUMI

Bones join as a human skull
with hollows left for the eyes. Space

for that second look Eros offered
forever-over-the-shoulder Orpheus.

Nothing to dwell on as he walked
through empty meadows—

homeward carriage of the body
back from a foreign land.

One of the First Questions

in the desert is how a rented house, some crows, and sprigs of spring
lilac can make it into my head, then out again as language—never mind
the stranger's bed I sleep in and mirrors full of moonlight.
                                                                 Even when
settled with a beer at dusk to study colors on a paint chart, I'm at a loss.
Add to that the apparition of my neighbor rising before dawn to water
and hum to her weeds. Blanket pulled over my head, I snarl.
                                                                        The dog
with a rhinestone collar doesn't disappoint me. She falls into stanzas.
Suz is always Suzie—asleep by the mailbox or chasing cars
up the dirt road.
                    I walk that road out to the abandoned chapel with the
crucifix and outhouse behind it. Those three structures have been here
longer than anyone cares to remember: hooded men still come to whip
themselves and moan like ghosts each Easter. These, the *pentitentes*, know
just who crucified the natives. They wail and labor in their dreams. Beyond
that memory comes the long view—Pueblo land all the way past Sacred
Mountain.
                    I write into sun-up or gray days, drag these five notebooks—
as if they were the ocean floor—for anything resembling my muse.
Fragments of fragments she can feed me, leaf stain from the adobe walls.
Imposter, she whispers, *this is not your land.* I cannot find my voice, the broom,
or even the hose they said was looped in the rafters. The off-button on the
alarm clock escapes me after the neighbor stops watering, and I doze.

But let's get back to that initial question of how to settle into another's
scented space—a big problem until early one Friday I recognize the
wind at my screen door, then the familiar clap of pigeon wings, forty
of them lifting twenty birds. And by afternoon burrs thicken my socks
from scavenging the plain again all day.
                                            I know these scratches as well
as I do the cemetery caretaker who glares an *off-with-you* then slams his
door. Because of my regular appearances among the graves, I am rebel-
liously at home. A squatter of sorts. Soon the outhouse and chapel seem
mine too. Wafts of ancient odor rise with grasshoppers
in the heat.

Only later do I understand that the greater part of transmutation comes with restlessness as coyote howl creeps into my bed along with the moon. Bark and bay in a chill blue light. I too vibrate with what's alive in the desert at dark.

My last hours here, an ant crawls diagonally across the blank page, and three Bosc pears want to be jammed in at the end: *skewed models of balance*, I scribble, then zip the stuffed red fox in my bag—lost ancestor for the baby girl at home. And also to take back, the fresh blue wing tattooed on my left ankle. Small and solitary, it's an energy that wobbles.

Easter Inventory

> —Easter falling on the first full moon after the
> Vernal Equinox allowed nomadic pilgrims
> enough light to travel by.

Stillness in the moonlit mirrors—
one marked *out*, the other

deeper into wander.

Hunger and fast fill the blue emptiness
of 4 a.m.   Who am I to question space

in someone else's double bed, sectioned off
for me and god knows what next phantom?

Coyote howls in the desert. Half asleep,
I mumble, *wily move*, drawn to the tremors

of another.

~

Drought, and magpies fly through the cottonwoods—
carnival magic on a stick, these raucous birds in black

and white. Two magpies are hand-painted on the sheet
beneath my pillow,
                mythic birds of happiness flattened
in the linens.

Footsteps under the window at night tell me the neighbor's
at it again. Humming, she hoses wither called her garden.

A tale, I think, is due this dark lady—the one that ends, *And,
as always, thirty thirsty magpies peck apart the sleepless creature
with her fat hose of desert water.*

~

Sitting in the backyard with paint-charts and a glass of beer,
I wonder how long that crow can blow about on the branch,

and not fly away. A young Korean lilac roots in arid soil,
crow flickers in the leaves, and the air's so dry it glitters—

my eyes so parched, they're hard to close. At sunset, I give
the birdbath two cups of water and a chunk of quartz carried

back from the canyon switchback. In town, the drummer calls
the hungry in for supper. There'll be no crow to judge when

this branch is empty, and I return to the colors between *ocean cloud* and *deep seashell*.

~

If the National Wildlife Fund hadn't sent me the toy barn owl
as a thank-you for my donation, I might not recognize what calls

from these tree. But I had squeezed that bird each night so my cat
could hear its *who-who*—two short then two long.
                                                Now an owl
full of breath echoes at twilight. Vociferous kin, this bird whose
fund-raising twin slept with my cat for months in a house only feet
from the Eastern Divide.   You think this an exaggeration? I know
my old backyard and how far sound travels.

~

April on the back road to the Penitentes Cemetery where the dusty
lilacs bloom. By evening the stacked mailboxes are empty, and

beneath them, the napping dog takes time-out to chase a passing car,
or two. Most folks slow down, used to Suzie's habits. Quite a different

response from the sign nailed every three feet on the fence ahead:
NO TRESPASSING!!! There's even a huge one in red propped

against the chimney. As I walk by, a boy yells from the upstairs
window, *hey woman, we own this road, you know.* The holy land,

he mumbles, though in both directions people walk home with
groceries. I smile and pick lilacs through his fence for Suzie's sparkly

collar, then spill photos from my folder of the big black crucifix
this side of Pueblo land and Sacred Mountain.　　At dark

my plane careens towards chimneys in dream,　　then stops
suddenly for a moment　　above Suzie asleep in the dust.

～

Four windows of the chapel are boarded up, and it's hard to find
a door or to get the story straight about who first crucified
the natives—
　　　　　generations flayed themselves for countless
holy weeks into the future.　History's long lineage
of penance

Yesterday when asked about that term *morado*, the cab driver looked
right at me, and said that was not his people's language,　　and
drove a whole lot faster.

Now　here's the chapel, its old crucifix, and outhouse
with three holes in a rotted plank.　　　　　Number the years
backwards to when the body finally was nailed, and soldiers
emptied their stomachs under the Easter moon.

Dodge/Luhan, Works in Progress

Eighty years, and Tony's pigeon houses sit on tall posts
in the courtyard. Three stories high, these ghosts of summer
dachas are for the common bird—portals under a shingled roof,
galleries to shit and strut upon.

Flocks fly the sunlit mountains.   Pale clouds of flight
part of the story Tony saw. And months later he hammered
in the last cold nail then walked home through the snow.

Carpenter for the birds, builder of Mabel's bedroom,
high and facing north. Always she'd look at his mountain.

Her plot's overgrown with weeds at the public cemetery.
Unremarkable. No wrought-iron fence around it.
                                        And Tony,
he's buried on Pueblo land near Blue Lake, sacred water
at the top of Taos Mountain. Proof of intervention,
of invention—sleeping place for a wife,
and another for the birds.

Materialism

In sleep my first home appears,
its insides confused with time running out
the doors and windows.

Each clock stopped at a different spectral point.

Essences attract me, starting with the striated eastern sky,
then moving into morning in the box canyon. Perhaps that's why
I took his dare to sleep with the glyph meaning flick-of-a-gecko's
tongue: pleasure that starts from within, wind making cartwheels
of the sand.

Beside me on the boulder is a line of vertebrae. Tiny spine—
a creature no longer. I too am without direction, feckless and sunning
on a rock.

Around the pool at lunch they do the desert thing, piped-in water
misting us like heads of grocery lettuce.
                                          Two guys splash about with beer,
yelling this is the worst motel pool they've hit all week—freeloaders
ready to vanish at a moment's notice, six-packs stacked in the rusty
pickup.

I give up on George by 5 o'clock, the African Gray in the breezeway.
He will not stop talking. Any syllables caught on the fly, this parrot
repeats without reflection.
                          Now he's a screeching eagle gliding through
the arroyo.
           Raspy voice of a solitary in the sky, the real eagle on TV
finishing its 200 mph descent after a rabbit.

What doesn't want to live inside the music of another? Take that shadow
this morning deep in Boynton Canyon. It circled splits of hematite,
me scurrying beneath in the red dirt.
                                The bloody earth, I thought,
while a mockingbird traded songs one at a time. Sort of like George,
who, upside down on his swing, keeps yelling, *Hands off, you dirty
lowdown two-timer.*

The Forest People

The twig house had nubs of wool for the stick-folk
to sleep upon; under the trees as a child I made life
breathe at my fingertips, home lit on the bluff
in drizzle.

Later when I had a small one of my own, and he could
not draw firm lines—ghost halloos, his own cobbled
pictures—disappointment rose.

I topped his hand with mine, saying, *this way, my way* until
his fingers locked. I must have wanted the perfect round
mouth and empty eyes of space.

vi. *such a baffled look as the beast lay stepped from.   Almost forgotten*

Mitosis

It was a year to the day that she bathed and started
the long division, following it back along the creek
outside his window, then down a gravel road
to the coastal highway.
                        And here came an eighteen-wheeler's
horn again   the brakes   her driving like crazy to find him

her son. Her almost late-phenomena she spotted alive and
standing in a filthy doorway. Her womb.   His eyes

on hers, and it struck   how she'd not checked on him
since childhood—absent   from his cells' dark busyness.

Under the skin   such heaviness   and the same
heart he had from the start.

Dark and Secret Kin

> Fire burn; and caldron bubble (said she) . . .
> how now, you secret black and midnight hags?
> (demanded he)
> —MACBETH

Halloween night on the ridge. In fact, my yard is on the Eastern
Divide, rivers flowing off to the Mississippi or east to the ocean.

But these diaries have the years cornered and ready to torch
in a wash tub—pages that will not ignite in the wind. Heavy

and gray in the garden, St. Francis stares. A few squirts of fire-
starter, and swoosh, up goes the past like the freshly bombed,

or my puny words in a metal bucket. Gusts pick out and throw
phases of me in my face. Goblin-breath on the coals, the hillside

flushes red with the venom of lovers. Wadded paper I poke
in the fire, passages of anger, of lust. Heat enough to recall

numberless newborns dumped in ditches—an occasion far
older than records, than anyone's diaries. *She*, the culprit; *her*,

a singular arraignment. Now one side of the union we wanted
burns wildly. I smack it with stones from under the bushes,

that close am I to toads and salamanders. Each tree lights up,
one fully grown woman hopping around her kettle of trouble.

No *eye of newt* or *lip of Tartar* to cast a spell on this finalé. Last
to go, my practice goodbye-letters. Sheaves of them broil. Tissue

of the vacuous, hiccupping, and incoherent.

Burnt October

1.
diaries   my declawed
denatured   brushes with intimacy

2.
slurred   frayed
words   centered on *not*

3.
we began   (and finished)
as a question   in part

4.
point of origin   (perfectly) limited
     half-life of two

5.
assumed   if at first we couldn't
we cannot

6.
and you   kept saying   *of course*
I know it (every bit)   my territorial insult

7.
equidistant   parallel lives   rattling on
without end

8.
stop/go/wait   another few
days   years

9.
who's to move   squirm   leave

10.
our house   partitioned
(postwar) entity

11.
tissue shaved   from the congested we

12.
listening   *time for what's said*   whoever
heard that heard wrong

13.
blame   taking/at   root

14.
given   we're all we know
small private collections

15.
subtexts   rise   squabble
hey now   say that again

16.
talk   not a sunlit   (pre)occupation

17.
I am   that I   logistically am

18.
time's up   the bottom line

19.
dawn   crimson smeared   sinking
    sleep   the escape route

20.
term for not wonder   *you*   in italics

21.
another   dizzying rejoinder   billows

22.
your proverbial ship   coming   almost
but not quite

23.
sailing   inevitably on

24.
red-rimmed   stomped   horizon

25.
who's to   jump ship   bridge our star-crossed
puddle

26.
numerical fact   two proven impossibilities
you   me

27.
chalk it up   figures
screech on teacher's blackboard

28.
crosshairs   steady now   calibrate
:   how could you have done

29.
did it

30.
transgressions   vermilion visions
     catch fire   flit

31.
October   the end of this
ghost mouth   at the window   moist

The Earth Flashed, *Fire Here*

Oxygen, layers of cells hungry to make
more of themselves. The skull spun
round for millennia, its gray
matter prepared.

Breaths lengthened.   Time deepened.

Small ones hang close to mother and her quick
warning nudges.
                The imagined was starting to hatch
in an unwieldy head with its great eyes.

Such a baffled look as the beast lay stepped from,
almost forgotten.

Earth flashed, *fire here, kill over there*. Then the pond
put a face on it, eyes jumpy with reflection.
The brow cramped,
                    lines set the wind could not
countermand.

Brief home for some or frail web to die in.

Hubris

November is a time to be faceless,
the treasury of bee energy stashed away.

How can the unknown play hide and seek
with the scent of another? Breath of nutmeg

on the strong autumn wind. And which lover's
tall bones were those that had her detach and

disrobe until tonight when she's face to the ground
like a bride doll, or novice—lace veil to her waist?

Maybe even a fully fledged nun. However you look
at it, she hides from the inside out. She smells of

concealment, of ashes and must, the stars hang
above her. The cold bites. It chews on her fingers

as if she were the remains of bright Bridgette tossed
out to freeze—goddess lamenter, mistress of fire

with the wild Irish hair. Or perhaps she's old Cailleach
too tired to budge after All Hallows—winter hag

each man must know lying down. Such diminished kin
for young women to choose from. Nun, bride, or crone,

she's queen of what's lacking—without god, love, or
a firm body. Wind blows from the north, the spirit-count

rising. Third season of the year is almost complete, altar set
on the rim. Saucer of coral in honey. Sage burns for the tally—

the night-watch for humans begun. And geologically speaking,
it's not been so long since the Tertiary Period arrived. Reptiles

declining, the mammals ascending. Tectonic rifts slip,
shift a fossil-jammed strata. Such hubris, our need for naming.

And here she lay on the veiled universe.

Black Roses

Traveling alone, I look for ways to frame the imperative.
Yesterday the sign on a gate scribbled in purple: *Please*

do not let my GUARD DOG SNEAK up on you! THANKS.
Since I'd had it with coy exaggeration, that invisible dog

was declassified and switched to substance neither to be
feared or trusted. Time to improvise, change life

to an entity only dimly suggestive of itself.   Shimmers
in well water.   Radial rebirth.

For instance, take that night I couldn't identify what came
from behind, whispering, *Take this picture with a zoom lens,*

but delete the broken roses in my veins. Breath of wine, mind
on slaughter—images that morph in dream: his familiar mouth

around me, feeding on tenderness and the chickens whose necks
he was trained to wring. Try coming up with a name for that one—

root-nuzzler at dawn before collapsing into the hide of another.
Even now, I smell the tracks of the enemy and press my hand

to the cliff, yelling, *Halt!* water bubbling through the red dirt
at my feet.   Steady now, these five fingers I raise usually

stay put, or given latitude they may fly off to more slippery
dimensions.   Remember the glyph we saw that meant two,

and how *time on my hands and you in my arms*   was a dark
transfusion.

Perspective

Mix of salt, lime, and the sun in the ocean—
our moment to walk the earth a bit closer.

Fledgling flagellants coalesce in the algae. Life
adds up and reaches out, its elephantine grasp
of the future begun.

From a marsh, the whatnots rise flailing. Blossoms,
the grain gold enough to make a wooly herbivore's
fat marble.

Not long before the flesh-eaters catch on, claw and
tooth ready to rip, ready to pick up the pace as down
through the leaves comes our simian host.

And one tree makes the whole sky seem lower.

vii   *who cares if the mouth has a beak   or bells in the throat*

The Silence

of closets and attics
of men's other wives
and sandbags on levees;

of his starry night
of her crawl space
and the whispered reverse;

of searchlights
of broken bone
and hair on a spade;

of tracks in the sand garden
of churches most days and nights
a song gone that went

breathe with the birds, and let wrath dissipate.

—after Theodore Roethke

A Light Sleeper

Repeat, *I am child of earth and the starry heaven.*
Lift those words from a thin sheet of gold inscribed for the dead
in the Aegean.
                    On the sea floor little ones
beneath a window of water.
                                  And here it comes that bright
vertiginous bundle of angel.

Mother-of-pearl with the wings swimming loose.
Babies drowse in watery wholeness—
big angel dropping down
above such
sleepy
minutia.

First among the thousands of the backlit forms that defy
possession.
           Flux angels thrive in.

When a child turns to ash   flecks of the featureless
blow through the pass at White Mountain.
                                        Exhaled,
each human foible.

Who cares if the mouth comes with a beak or bells in the throat?
Children know how the world takes place

Tall sea with its undeclared edges

Rilke had angels and young ghosts like that   Pale shudder
over the crib
                And there's that morsel with the promising
elflike ears   a light sleeper

Coastal Epithalamion

It was probably a rainy afternoon south of the lake,
east of the marsh when you were conceived. Beyond

any hope or need, your journey begins. There you
are, my fresh embryo with the amber lantern lit.

Cells of the heart spin,   first property of life.
Heart-first you bend into time. Had I

dreamed you since birth?   I mean since my own
beginning, had I sensed those intricacies of nerve

and bone and skin. Your flex.   But look at you
now among the grapevines, weddings
old as wine itself.
                  Toast the patience of pale and
scarlet fruit—a long wait too that brought this
woman to find   the wedding inside you.

See now your bride approaches near the sea

and time   moves   slowly   and clearly
as it   ever will   Something

loosening   loosens   in the tropics

where a deeper world comes through

                                  —for Lauren and Ashton

Fuzz

We eat amaranth porridge with butter
at a table on the deck. Deer in the bushes
crunch then gulp almost-whole apples
one at a time.

The woman across from me tries hard
to swallow. Amaranth is first to flower
after destruction.

Red blossom in the rubble.

Hot cereal is soft in my mouth. The throat
near me struggles. Fuzz on a deer's antlers.
Towers explode and collapse. Humans
come to nothing.

Some awareness is choiceless,
not a story.

Simplicity

Low down and blue as the sky is up and endlessly out there,
I lie naked on my balcony in the sun. The cat purrs beside
his bowl of water, garbage truck grinding
up the mountain.

I've sewn a bluebird wing on the kite, my skirt
hemmed and folded beside me as a helicopter dips
overhead. I could be a sleeping snapshot of beauty,
each of her tasks complete.

The pyracantha hedge grows taller around me.
In mid-thought, I'm walled in and put down
for a hundred-year nap.
Breathing slows
and the house becomes transparent,
more like a vase layered with cloud.
I fade to sepia, then to the shade
that won't wear off.

That April the rock garden was my refuge. Ocean stones
I placed around the concrete garden saint that stood by a dozing,
broken-hipped deer. Reports of you came from miles away—
certificate ready concerning one no longer here.

Aerial Photo-Ops of the Biome

:

Above strata of fossilized coral, the condor flies
as it did sixty million years ago
                              when no digital distancing
could make life look hazy. Should I sink farther into my bath
water or head for the canyon ledge, bloody rabbit in hand?
Full-frontal view of anthropoid time—
my snowy robe parted.

:

Humans wander far below as they have for the past
month, or so, focusing on the dominant range of colors
in their world.
                Pistachio, medium rare, Pacific-fusion green,
sugar blues. Espresso mean. A boy gulps a bottle of Jolt,
then charges the ice cream stand, shrieking.

:

Ninety years ago my grandfather appeared to be and
was truthfully in the process of leaving the family.
He locked his front door, and was next spotted
years from there selling cars in Kansas City.
Sound of small change. Gold ring of keys,
and heavy men with soft cowhide wallets.

Point, Line, and Plane

Smoke curls from the mesa while my inky blue lines
connect. Good to finish with words by evening—*leaks
of russet and clockwork folded into strata*—

                                              stop

the mind in its tracks.

Other than fossils, are there traces of what left eons ago?
Our adumbrated past.

Proof of plumped geometries, summer grasses with auras
blowing in the sun furnace, mirage of ghost shirts dancing
after the fires go out.

Take the way   I just nodded to my own question,
Does anything remain? Agreeable, my small gesture,

while deeper underground, the shades realign.

Shadowland of Hades, this canyon we think can't falter.

At dusk, I want what's solid to stay. Euclid thought like that
with his constellations of lines, rays, and segments. Locked
right-angles.

Certainties only a brain concocts.

At dark I wander off   like a nomad to the canyon edge
Solitary   stars
farther away than oceans of luminous foam.

Counterpoint, the Milky Way, with me beneath and too far gone
with thoughts of another.

I hold my finger to the moon so the lunar field grows slight.

Yesterday a stretch of darkness shrank to split-in-the-high-plateau,
then closer (and from a bridge) I watched the river churn
hundreds of feet below.
$\qquad\qquad\qquad\qquad$ My pelvis, a vast unsteadiness—vase of plenty
of nothing above the Rio Grande. The wind, centrifugal and indivisible,
sent my scarf flying.

A good book I have says there was soft (sandstone) then hard matter.
Old spirits (condor, elemental shiver of dragonfly)   and countless
names for affliction.

Filthy, rich, and random, Earth is more than a curve we walk on.

Note: *subaqueous* is followed by *sub-arid* in the dictionary—
the time it takes to get from a cool river bottom
to the desert.

Lake Itasca is the headwaters of the Mississippi. Currents
of wet brown sequins, alluvium washing
south.

The Good Book routes ways to and from kingdom-come.
The best/worst part of the trip depends on point of view.

Vision.

Long line of lotus at Buddha's birthday altar.

Offspring.   The word estriol (female sex hormone)
is rooted in thee*lol*   (Grk. *female* + Latin. *oil*).

Oil of woman, fecund and humid.   In (and out of) heat.

Geologic time—eon era   epoch   *Kaibab* always is
Hopi for mountain-lying-down

Geomancy: peak   lagoon   divination of brimstone

dust

time blowing

across the plains   grasses   so tall

the human figure looks pointless

Introduction

I have happy childhood memories of Christmas at the residence of my aunt and uncle at Norton, Yorkshire. You could not walk far along the village without hearing the clucking of hens, the lowing of pigs - and imbibing the smells which went with them. Cottages and farms were randomly sited along the village street, and I regarded Norton as the quintessential English village. The area around Norton abounded in delightful walks, which we took advantage of on many an Easter Monday. The weather was always glorious. One day, having watched a cricket match at Askern, we walked back to Norton via Askern Colliery, in whose offices my uncle worked. I was reminded that there were more than pretty villages in the region.

My aunt and uncle, Annie and Edwin Hulme, lived in a modern semi called Westville on the west side of Norton. One of their friends, George Watson, lived part way down the village in a house with a smallholding and orchard at the rear. He kept chickens, geese and pigs, plus a Jack Russell and several cats. George, a tall good-looking man, was a bachelor. His day job was delivering sacks of coal from Askern Colliery on his lorry. George could barely read or write, but his business acumen, especially concerning livestock, was second to none. My uncle did George's bookkeeping. On several occasions, I went with my father and George to Doncaster market in his truck. George was adept at bidding for chickens or geese, and sometimes pigs.

The halcyon days of childhood over, I started work in 1946 and took a part-time course in engineering. I learned about iron and steel production and became familiar (on paper) with blast furnaces and Bessemer steel. A coach was hired to take us on an evening trip to the Park Gate Iron & Steel Company at Rotherham, where we saw first-hand the manufacture of iron and steel. I watched molten iron being transferred from the huge blast furnaces to metal mixers and then to open-hearth furnaces. I saw molten steel being extracted from the furnaces to make ingots. Passing through various cogging mills, these eventually became round, square or hexagonal bars. Workmen seemed to be scurrying in all directions, but every employee knew exactly what he was doing. Finished products included pit props and pit arches. We were provided with a meal before returning to Wakefield.

In 1968, I travelled overnight by train to Cornwall on holiday. Passing the Rotherham area as darkness fell, I saw the flashing reflections created by the many steel furnaces, and flames leaping from chimneys as waste gases were burned off. Returning two weeks later in daylight, I knew I had reached South Yorkshire when I saw the pit heaps, the overhead conveyors for dumping waste and the collieries themselves. These seemed to tell me that South Yorkshire's industries were as vibrant as ever and had a future. How wrong I was!

Many kitchen drawers once contained cutlery made in Sheffield. I still have (and occasionally use) some of those bone-handled knives from the 1930s with 'Stainless steel' and 'Made in Sheffield' inscriptions. The making of cutlery used to be a cottage industry, with the master, his journeymen and apprentices dealing with all the processes. The workmen later gathered in factories where each did a particular specialised job. Pocket knives needed many hands to produce the individual parts, such as cutting the bone, making the brass fittings or hardening, forging and grinding the blades. Grinders were prone to suffer from grinders' asthma, especially after the introduction of steam grinding wheels from 1876 onwards. This pulmonary affliction could be fatal. In the early 1900s, in spite of Factory Acts to minimise the dust evil, mortality among grinders remained high.

Sheffield became the world's great cutlery mart, but saws and files were also

(continued)

produced. File cutting by hand was an injurious operation, leading to a disease called plumbism, a kind of lead poisoning. This was caused by swallowing and inhaling particles of dust from the leaden bed upon which the files were placed while being cut. With the introduction of machine file cutting, the disease became less prevalent. Hand file cutting had almost disappeared by 1910.

Visitors to Sheffield's Meadowhall shopping complex or Don Valley Stadium may not realize that these were erected on ground once dedicated to the city's great iron and steel industry. While some smaller works were located near the city centre, the heavier industry extended northeast along the banks of the River Don, the Sheffield & Tinsley Canal and the later Midland Railway goods line. Here were found the big Cyclops Iron & Steel Works, the Park Iron Works and the Grimesthorpe Steel Works, to name a few. Sheffield's steel industry gained momentum from the 1850s onwards. Among the pioneers who gave their names to successful firms were John Brown, Thomas Firth, Charles Cammell and Edward Vickers.

The pictures herein, all taken from postcards in my collection, represent South Yorkshire at its industrial peak. Steel, coal and their related activities feature strongly. Less distinguished but necessary tasks such as delivering milk, sweeping the road or working in a laundry also feature. The industries helped to establish towns or villages and create communities. When the rolling mills and the coal mines went, some of the camaraderie of life, both at work and in the community, was lost. Perhaps forever!

Cammell Laird and its Postcards

Charles Cammell, born in Hull, came to Sheffield in 1830, aged 21. For a while he worked for Ibbotson Brothers at the Globe Steel Works on Penistone Road, where files, saws, railway springs, nuts and bolts were made. In 1837, he left the firm and, along with Thomas Johnson, founded the firm of Johnson, Cammell & Company in Furnival Street, Sheffield, making steel implements, including files. New premises were erected on open fields in Savile Street and named the Cyclops Works. Johnson died in 1852 and the firm became Charles Cammell & Company in 1855. It rapidly expanded, acquiring blast furnaces, mines and collieries along the way. It took over the Grimesthorpe Steel, Tyre & Spring Works at Sheffield, the Yorkshire Steel & Iron Works at Penistone, a couple of iron works in Cumberland and the Old and New Oaks Collieries at Barnsley. An advertisement for 1902 included the manufacture of steel rails, marine and locomotive castings and forgings, armour plates, propeller shafts, springs, buffers and files. In 1903, Cammell & Company amalgamated with Laird Brothers, the Birkenhead shipbuilding firm, to become Cammell Laird & Company. It eventually became part of the British Steel Corporation.

During the 1914-18 War, Cammell Laird issued three sets of coloured art postcards depicting interior scenes of their steelworks. These comprised two sets of seven cards and one set of six. The sets were supplied in envelopes. A double-humped camel, which had become the company's trademark, was printed on the envelopes and the backs of the cards. Also printed on the backs were dates when the pictures were passed by censor. Some of the scenes are specific to wartime, but most of them represent activities which could apply to peacetime. The illustrations were also used for brochures. A representative nine of the postcards feature in this book.

Norman Ellis
November 2006

3. The lively scene shows stone quarries at Green Moor, near **Huthwaite**, to the west of Wortley. Blocks of stone and flat slabs are visible, as are cranes and a small tramway. The card, by Biltcliffe of Penistone, was posted from Wortley in June 1910.

4. From quarries at Levitt Hagg, **Warmsworth**, Doncaster, lime was extracted by Lockwood, Blagden & Crawshaw. This later became Yorkshire Amalgamated Products. Some of the lime was used in the iron and steel industry. The lime burning house is at near right. The River Don, railway and a scarred landscape are evident on this postcard by J Simonton & Son.

5. An employee of the **Sheffield** Cleansing Department helps to keep the city's streets clean. The donkey looks on sardonically, having just made extra work for his master!

6. The **Sheffield** Model Dairy, one of whose floats is shown c.1907, advertised pasteurised milk as early as 1902. Milkmen took the milk around to homes, where it was poured via a pint or half-pint ladle into the customer's jug or basin, for storage in a cellar or on a pantry stone.

7. Side by side at Meadow Head, **Woodseats**, Sheffield, are the premises of John Codd, joiner and wheelwright, and (with outside stairway) those of William Archer, shoeing and general smith. One dealt with the client's cart; the other with the motive power. Morgan & Sons, Sheffield, produced the card, c.1910.

8. A pair of leather-aproned blacksmiths pause at Albert Bly's shoeing forge at Spring Vale. The cart belonged to F Hague of Common Side, Crookes. These areas were two miles west of **Sheffield** centre.

9. *"The market overflows into the open air, and the square is crowded with stalls, where rosy-cheeked country-women display their eggs, butter and chickens, and traders from neighbouring areas bring their wares for sale"* - **Doncaster** Homeland Handbook, 1925. This card of Doncaster Market, posted in 1904, captures the atmosphere admirably.

10. Men with sticks seem intent on keeping order at **Doncaster** Market. The animals, chickens and other produce were reminders of the hardworking agricultural and farming communities in surrounding areas. The card, by J Crowther Cox of Rotherham, was posted in 1908.

11. Denaby was best known for its colliery, but Kilner Brothers established a glass works there, specialising in bottles. Part of the Great Central Railway line is visible in the foreground, with a siding leading into Kilner's. The card was posted in 1917.

12. Pilkington Brothers, makers of plate glass at St Helens, Lancashire, purchased an estate at **Kirk Sandall**, near Doncaster, in about 1920. There they built a huge manufactory, plus a model village for workers, to expand their plate glass production. This Scrivens postcard shows the huge factory.

13. With a farming past, **Wath-upon-Dearne** became industrialized, with collieries, a soap and manure manufactory, and a brewery. Gas lighting came to its streets in 1845 and a local gas board was formed in 1908. The gasworks are pictured on Station Road, c.1910, on a card by J Crowther Cox.

14. In 1793, George Newton and Thomas Chambers leased land from Earl Fitzwilliam at **Thorncliffe** (between Barnsley and Sheffield) on which to build an ironworks. The works are shown c.1910, with Thorncliffe Wood behind. The two blast furnaces on the left were constructed in 1874, to replace two earlier ones.

15. The Newton Chambers empire included this drift mine, begun in 1859 near the ironworks at **Thorncliffe** and seen here c.1910. The site included a large number of coke ovens, one of the by-products from these being Izal disinfectant.

16. This shows the boiler shop at **Thorncliffe** Works with a blurb for the famous Izal. The name was registered in 1893. Newton Chambers started to produce toilet paper in the 1920s, medicated with Izal and carrying pictures and text to extol it. The card, by Lamb of Barnsley, was posted from Chapeltown in 1914.

Low forge Wortley nr Sheffield

17. Throughout history, until 1929, iron was forged at **Wortley**. The forge was situated by the River Don, one mile east of Wortley village, itself ten miles northwest of Sheffield. The card, posted from nearby Huthwaite Lane in August 1913, shows various forgings scattered about the works yard.

18. This card of **Wortley** Forge has a message written on 22 June 1910 from Jack to Mary: *"I think the forge is playing next week, they are taking the stock."* However, the billowing smoke indicates work in progress. The forge became well-known for the manufacture of railway axles.

19. In 1862-63, Benson, Adamson & Garnett erected iron and steel works in **Penistone**. In 1864, the firm was purchased by Charles Cammell & Co, later to become Cammell Laird & Co. Here the huge works form a backdrop to Penistone Station on a card posted in 1910. Works and station have been demolished.

20. The Park Gate Iron & Steel Co was established at **Rotherham** in the 1820s. This pair of new blast furnaces was erected in 1905. Each was capable of producing up to 2,000 tons of iron per week. It was run into ladles for transfer to other departments.

21. The expansion of **Stocksbridge**, nine miles west of Sheffield, was due to rich deposits of coal, clay and ganister (for lining furnaces). The development of the brickworks was surpassed by the coming of the steelworks of Samuel Fox, shown to right of centre c.1922. The card was produced by R Smith of Sheffield for Abson's local stationery shop.

22. With an imposing facade, part of the **Stocksbridge** works of Samuel Fox & Co are illustrated, c.1905. The firm, once employing 7000 people, made many kinds of steel, and produced rails, springs and umbrella frames.

SHEFFIELD.
from The Victoria Hotel.

"JOTTER"

23. This is one of a series of six postcards of **Sheffield**, published by Raphael Tuck & Sons in their *Oilette* series. The set, numbered 7676, is titled *Work-a-day Sheffield*, the artist being Jotter (Hayward Young). This view, from a window of the Victoria Hotel, near the Great Central Railway station, shows Blonk Bridge crossing the River Don. On the right, backing on to the water, is Samuel Osborn's Clyde Steel & Iron Works, with the pinnacles of Sheffield Castle beyond. The spire of St Marie's Church and the tower of the Town Hall are visible in the distance. Three further postcards from the set feature on the next two pages.

24. Early morning and a vast pall of smoke hangs over the murky River Don. The development of **Sheffield** owed much to the Don and its navigations. It provided power, supported cargoes and carried the area's effluent.

25. The tramcar on the left is passing along Nursery Street, Wicker, **Sheffield**, near Trinity Church. Visible on the opposite bank of the Don are the Millsands Works, with forging and rolling mills. Both these postcards are from Tuck *Oilette* set 7676.

Sunset and Smoke, Sheffield.

26. *"Many of the forges and works have small outbuildings erected on piles driven into the bed of the river. Grimy as these buildings are, they form picturesque groups, and at sunset their sordid details are softened and glorified by the evening glow"* runs the caption on the reverse of this Tuck *Oilette* postcard, part of set no. 7676. The Don is shown from Lady's Bridge, **Sheffield**, with the Patent Piston Works on the left.

27. The Doncaster family came to **Sheffield** from Maplebeck in Nottinghamshire. Da
converter, with furnaces in Copper Street. Further premises were acquired in Sheffiel
and Hoyle Street. Some of their input was high quality Swedish iron. Their advertising
the Sheffield trade kept in stock for immediate delivery." Their fleet of wagons becan
city. Behind the slightly-bulged steamer, with its 'undertype' boiler, is a smaller Guy t

arted as a file maker and steel
ncaster Street, Penistone Road
d "Regular sizes of steel to suit
miliar sight in and around the
ith a Sheffield registration.

BENDING ARMOUR PLATE UNDER 12,000 TON PRESS.   CAMMELL LAIRD. SHEFFIELD

28. On a postcard issued by Cammell Laird of **Sheffield** during the 1914-18 War, armour plate is being bent under a 12,000 ton press. Through the entry on the right stands a small locomotive.

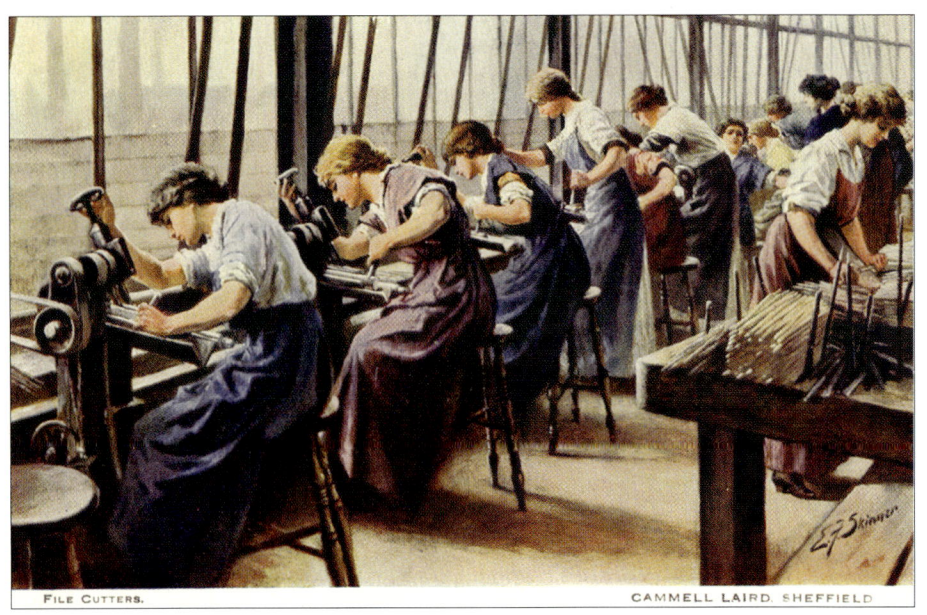

FILE CUTTERS.   CAMMELL LAIRD. SHEFFIELD

29. At Cammell Laird, **Sheffield**, young ladies (without any head protection!) are cutting files with the aid of machines, after forging and heat-treating for hardening.

COILING AND SETTING SPRINGS.   CAMMELL LAIRD, SHEFFIELD

30. Workmen exert appropriate caution with the coiling of springs at Cammell Laird, **Sheffield**. A coiling machine is pictured in the background, while a quenching tank is on the right.

FITTING LAMINATED SPRINGS   CAMMELL LAIRD, SHEFFIELD

31. *"Many hands make light work"* but a good deal of expertise was needed in the making of laminated springs at Cammell Laird, **Sheffield**. The sections were made red hot in the furnace at the back before being beaten to shape. Demand for coil and laminated springs for road and rail vehicles was on the increase.

TURNING HEAVY SHELL. CAMMELL LAIRD, SHEFFIELD

32. During the 1914-18 War, many **Sheffield** firms such as Cammell Laird were engaged in the supply of combat essentials. Here, heavy shells are being turned on lathes. This view was passed by the censor on 24 April 1917.

SHELL WORKERS. CAMMELL LAIRD, SHEFFIELD.

33. Women, who appear to be well kitted out with uniforms, including headgear, are working on smaller shells at Cammell Laird, **Sheffield**, during wartime. The picture was passed by censor on 21 December 1916.

34. Damsons are being gathered on Thomas Gravil's fruit farm at **Thorne** for Messrs Kenyon & Sons. The card was posted from Tom Gravil to Mr & Mrs C Rodway, 43 Clayfield Road, Mexborough, on 12 September 1906, with the message, *"Your fruit will be sent from Doncaster Saturday."*

35. Low lying land in the **Thorne** area yielded a good supply of peat for winter fuel. Later, it was used as animal litter and horticultural compost. The men are loading peats into wagons for conveyance along one of the moor tramways. The card was produced by the Regina Co of Doncaster.

36. A pair of heavy horses assists with haymaking at Footwalk Field, **Crookes**, on the northwestern outskirts of Sheffield. The card was posted from Sheffield to Ashton-under-Lyne on 19 August 1907 - an appropriate time for haymaking.

37. Henry Silvester, a grocer at **Hoyland Common**, stands proudly with his trusty horse and cart, a common sight in the area near Barnsley in the 1920s. His address was 75 Stead Lane. Henry had previously been a beer retailer at 78 Stead Lane. By the middle 1930s, the grocery business had been taken over by John Woodburn.

MEXBORO' CHIMNEY – 150 ft. High.
Erected for the Yorkshire Amalgamated Products Ltd., Conisboro' 1927
also demolition of old Chimney.

38. Yorkshire Amalgamated Products established a brick making plant on Doncaster Road, **Mexborough**. Here, in 1927, the old and new chimneys are shown side by side. The new chimney on the right has a round section; the older chimney to its left, with square section, is awaiting demolition. By the 1920s, brick had largely replaced the more-expensive stone for many building projects. The card was produced by Lilywhite.

39. The **Doncaster** Plant Works, a limb of the Great Northern Railway, was famous for the manufacture and repair of locomotives and carriages. During the 1914-18 War, women were employed there on the production of guns and shells. A group of them is shown on a card by the Regina Co of Doncaster.

40. Uniformed Midland Railway staff line up in front of an express parcels traffic wagon. The uncaptioned card was posted from Rotherham to Leicester in December 1906, and is believed to show the parcels depot at **Rotherham** Midland.

41. The wintry scene at **Kilnhurst** (Midland) Station, captured c.1905, shows the stationmaster and his staff with, in the distance, a man involved in snow clearance. This busy passenger station had sidings to various collieries and other works. It closed in 1968.

42. South-east of **Doncaster**, workmen pause outside Low Ellers Junction signal box on the South Yorkshire Joint Railway, while the signalman looks on. The railway, constructed in 1903-08, opened on 1 January 1909. The photograph probably dates from 1908.

43. The cut on the River Don at **Sprotborough** is shown c.1905, looking towards Doncaster. The horse-hauled barge has stopped beside the old water-powered flour mill on the right, which ceased production in the 1930s. Many of the barges carried coal to Hull and returned with corn.

44. Looking north from **Swinton** Bridge, two horse-drawn vessels pass on the Sheffield & South Yorkshire Navigation, c.1910. To the left, the Midland Railway wagons are a reminder that canal business was being lost to the railways. Swinton was noted for steel and glass production, also boatbuilding. A local stationer, CF Hurst, sold the postcard.

45. On the New Cut of the River Don, sailing keels are visible outside the elegant steam-powered corn mill of Thomas Hanley & Sons, Lower Fishergate, **Doncaster**. The hung washing on one keel suggests a family living on board.

46. A driver and conductor (with money bag and bell-punch machine) stand proudly beside their stylish omnibus. New in c.1929, it belonged to Halstead Brothers of Carlton, near **Barnsley**. Most employees went to work by tram, bus and train - or walked. For convenience, houses were often built close to workplaces.

47. Coal, from the colliery at **Askern**, is being bagged direct from a railway wagon, probably for home delivery, c.1927.

48. Following the ceremony of cutting the first sod on 23 October 1905, work began on constructing a colliery at **Brodsworth**. Some of the many men engaged in the work are pictured building the no.1 engine house and no.1 headgear. The card was posted from Doncaster in September 1908. The colliery closed in 1990.

49. Dearne Valley Colliery was a drift mine at **Little Houghton**, 5 miles east of Barnsley. Established in 1900-01, it is pictured a few years later. The two drifts were complemented by a vertical shaft, used for ventilation. At its peak, the colliery had an unusually high output. It closed in 1991.

50. Coal production at **Dinnington** Colliery commenced in 1906. It was followed by construction of coke ovens and brick making plant. Much of the complex is shown in this panoramic view, on a card produced by EL Scrivens of Doncaster. It was posted from Dinnington to Kirk Smeaton in 1923.

51. Bullcroft Colliery, near the village of **Carcroft**, was constructed between late 1909 and early 1912. Miners, some of them with lamps, are pictured in front of one of the lattice steel headstocks in 1912. Closure came in 1970.

52. Coal mines were plagued with explosions. Great heroism was shown by members of volunteer rescue teams in saving trapped comrades. Here, in the early 1920s, members of the Waleswood Colliery team present themselves in front of the **Rotherham** & District Rescue Station. Note the caged canary for detecting gas.

53. The premises of Woodhouse & Co, brassfounders of Urban Road, **Hexthorpe**, near Doncaster, suffered a disastrous fire at one o'clock in the morning. Glimpsing the damage are some of the 400 workmen who were laid off. The Scrivens card was posted on 10 October 1908 (17 days after the fire).

54. Workers at the wholesale market at Castle Folds in the centre of **Sheffield** had to rise very early. Fred Harrison was a fruit and flower merchant there for many years. Observe the scales, first aid cabinet and a notice for egg boxes.

440. "Doncaster Jossy." J.S.&S.

55. The knocker-up was a familiar figure in many northern towns. Doncaster Jossy, shown here on a card by J Simonton & Son of Balby, was the town's most famous. He arose extremely early and, with a 'drumstick', knocked on the doors or windows of **Doncaster** workers to ensure they were not late for work. Some knockers-up used a long pole with wires, or alternatively spokes from an old umbrella, on the end, to minimise damage to upstairs windows. Knockers-up were paid a small amount for their services. Doncaster Jossy, who sometimes dressed eccentrically, charged double if two or more workers in one house required his services.

56. The Woodview Domestic Laundry was situated on Woodview Road, **Walkley**, Sheffield. Its proprietor in the early 1900s was George A Milne.

57. This and the upper picture of Woodview Domestic Laundry, **Walkley**, probably date from c.1912. Some of the lady employees in the lower photograph look particularly young. The normal school leaving age from 1880 until 1918 was 13 years.

58. William Warman ran the Hope Street Bakery at **Mexborough**. His early model T Ford shows a West Riding registration. It was photographed by Maurice Medcalf, a photographer of High Street, Mexborough.

59. The owners of this T model Ford, with a Rotherham registration, were HM Adams & Son, wholesale and retail grocers and confectioners, with premises on Greasbrough Road and Greasbrough Street, **Rotherham**. The photograph was taken on 23 June 1916, with the lady doing her bit towards winning the war.